LIFE IN
Georgian
Britain
FROM 1700 TO 1837

Michael St John Parker

IMPORTANT DATES

1701 The Act of Settlement establishes the Hanoverian succession.

1704 The Battle of Blenheim and victory for the Duke of Marlborough.

1707 England and Scotland unite under one Parliament.

1712 Thomas Newcomen invents a steam engine.

1714 The death of Queen Anne; George of Hanover (son of Sophia, Electress of Hanover and grand-daughter of James I) becomes king of Great Britain.

1715 The first Jacobite rising, in support of James Edward Stuart, the Old Pretender.

1720 The South Sea Bubble financial scandal; Sir Robert Walpole is Britain's first 'Prime Minister'.

1727 George II succeeds his father, George I.

1745 The second Jacobite rising in support of Charles Edward Stuart, Bonnie Prince Charlie (the Young Pretender).

1756–63 The Seven Years' War with France.

1760 George III becomes king.

1764 James Hargreaves invents the 'spinning jenny' to speed up textile manufacture.

1769 James Watt designs an improved steam engine.

1770 James Cook lands in Australia during the first of three voyages of Pacific exploration.

1775 The war for American independence begins. By 1783 Britain has lost its American colonies.

1789–99 The French Revolution; by 1792 Britain is at war with France, a war that lasts more or less continuously until 1815.

1804 Richard Trevithick drives a steam carriage. Napoleon becomes Emperor of the French.

1805 The Battle of Trafalgar; Nelson dies at the moment of victory.

1807 The abolition of the slave trade in the British Empire.

1815 The Battle of Waterloo; Wellington and Blucher end Napoleon's hopes of returning to power.

1820 George III is succeeded by George IV, Prince Regent during his father's illness.

1830 William IV succeeds his brother, George IV.

1837 Victoria becomes queen.

INTRODUCTION

*I*N 1700, AS A NEW CENTURY DAWNED, few people in the British Isles could have felt optimistic about the future. Still fresh in many memories were the strife and rancour of the Civil War, and the Glorious Revolution of 1688–89. Queen Anne, last of the Stuart monarchs, reigned until 1714. The succession had been decided by Parliament in 1701 and on Anne's death, the crown duly passed to George of Hanover. So began the Georgian era.

From this uncertain beginning, Georgian Britain grew in wealth and power; trade, wars and voyages of exploration opened up new imperial vistas in Canada, India, Australia and the Pacific. In an age of elegance, epitomised by the landscapes of Capability Brown and the architecture of Adam and Nash, Georgian Britain also hummed with new ideas and energy. Breakthroughs in agriculture, industry and science laid the foundations for an industrial and social revolution that was to transform the nation. The 18th century proved a fortunate century for Britain: increasingly confident in the power of its navy and its industrial economy, proud of its liberties, and more assured of its unity. The Georgian dynasty survived the age of enlightenment and the turbulence of the American and French revolutions, to usher in the imperial and industrial dynamism of the Victorians. It was an age of high life and low life, every sort of extreme, splendour and sophistication: an age that left an elegant and entertaining legacy.

AN AGE OF REASON

WE CALL THE 18TH CENTURY the Georgian period simply because for most of that hundred years Britain was ruled by kings who were named George, but the adjective has also come to epitomise a culture.

Georgian Britain was economically prosperous, enterprising and sturdily self-sufficient; its politics were vigorous but essentially peaceable; its ruling aristocracy was preoccupied with the idea of liberty; its architecture, literature and art were all suffused with ideals derived from classical antiquity, but its religion was a stoutly Protestant, rather secular Christianity; its science was as rational and innovative as its manners were traditional and conservative. The lawyer William Blackstone described the British of his time as 'a polite and commercial people'.

Education was highly valued even though the schools and universities were in a torpid state. There was a remarkable growth in learned societies, such as the Royal Academy, the Royal Society of Antiquaries and the British Academy.

Not that the period was uniform in any way: it was marked by variety of every sort, a rich complexity that makes every generalisation risky. On the whole, though, it was a time when life was good for many people, and getting better for most, when it was easy to believe in the possibility of improvement, and when civilisation was understood to mean the ordering, rather than the altering, of nature.

BELOW: The Connoisseurs, *by David Allan. An informed interest in all branches of art and learning was a mark of sophistication; an art collection was an expression of the connoisseur's taste, rather than an investment.*

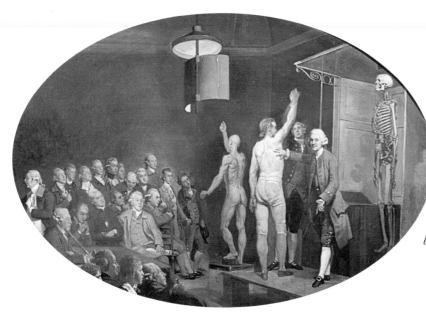

LEFT: *An anatomy lesson at the Royal Academy, depicted by Johann Zoffany. The century saw rapid advances in all the sciences, particularly in the various branches of biology.*

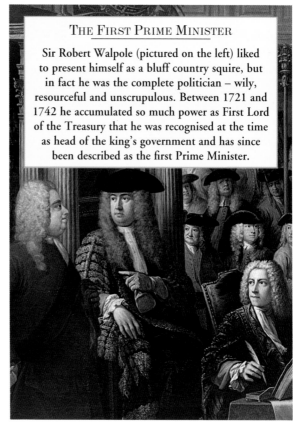

THE FIRST PRIME MINISTER

Sir Robert Walpole (pictured on the left) liked to present himself as a bluff country squire, but in fact he was the complete politician – wily, resourceful and unscrupulous. Between 1721 and 1742 he accumulated so much power as First Lord of the Treasury that he was recognised at the time as head of the king's government and has since been described as the first Prime Minister.

LEFT: *A portrait of the Brockman family at Beachborough, painted by Edward Haytley in the 1740s. Despite its formality, this picture of a rural idyll should not be dismissed as unreal: such elegant tranquillity was the 18th-century ideal.*

IN SAFE HANDS

QUEEN ANNE'S REIGN (1702–14) was marked by brilliant military successes against France, above all the stunning victory at Blenheim in 1704, and by a growth in the country's overseas trade, which laid the foundations for subsequent economic success. Although Anne had become pregnant 17 times, none of her children survived her and, on her death, the Crown passed to her nearest Protestant relative, George, Elector of Hanover. So a German dynasty came to reign in Britain, both to placate popular distrust of Roman Catholics and in accordance with the terms of the Act of Settlement of 1701 – the beginnings of constitutional monarchy.

George I (1714–27) and his son George II (1727–60) thought of themselves primarily as German rulers and they spent as much time as they could at home in Hanover; George I, indeed, spoke little English. They relied largely on the aristocracy of Britain to manage affairs for them, a policy which seemed to be justified by successful wars, imperial expansion and a rapid increase in national prosperity.

But when George III came to the throne in 1760, the Crown became embroiled in new constitutional controversies. He was keenly British, enthusiastically conscientious, and also all too

LEFT: George II was the last British king to lead his own troops into battle. On 27 June 1743, he defeated a French army at the Battle of Dettingen.

CONSTITUTIONAL MONARCHY

Under the Act of Settlement of 1701, if Queen Anne failed to produce an heir the succession was to be limited to another Protestant Stuart line, and all future sovereigns were to be members of the Church of England. The act was subtitled 'An Act for better securing the rights and liberties of the subject': it embodied principles, such as the independence of the judges from the Crown, that have proved of lasting importance to the development of the British Constitution.

willing to take sides at a time of rising difficulties both at home and abroad. In George III's later years, however, as the nation rallied together in struggle against revolutionary and Napoleonic France, the monarchy emerged as a symbol, not so much of national leadership, as of national unity. Ironically, during this period of growing royal popularity, the king suffered from severe bouts of mental illness.

ABOVE: Queen Charlotte, George III's wife, with two of her children. Johann Zoffany's portrait combines splendour with a certain charming informality, shown in the children's fancy dress and their mother's obvious affection.

ABOVE: The appearance of George III's image in popular art reflected his involvement in public affairs during the second half of the century.

LEFT: George III at the garden entrance to St James's Palace. The third Hanoverian king – a man of relatively domestic tastes – moved among his subjects with little fuss or formality.

PATRONAGE AND PRINCIPLE

POLITICAL ACTIVITY IN 18th-century Britain was intense, unscrupulous and frequently savage. The two main political groupings, known as Whigs and Tories, had much in common. Essentially, they were rival aristocratic factions, jostling each other ruthlessly for control of the source of political influence – the right to make effective appointments to profitable posts under the Crown. Those who could operate the system successfully held the levers of power, in the shape of the great offices of state which gave authority over public order, the defence of the realm and the conduct of foreign affairs, with all the opportunities for enrichment that inevitably followed.

Parliament provided the arena where this power-struggle took place. The party leaders were generally to be found in the House of Lords, which was in some respects, therefore, more important than the House of Commons. Elections to the Commons were infrequent – a seven-year rule applied for much of the century – and few people were qualified to vote. 'Patronage' – the giving or withholding of favours, particularly appointments to offices under the Crown – and outright bribery were the main considerations in securing political results, at all levels of the system.

In short, 18th-century Britain was far from being a democracy. Rather, it enjoyed a partially representative system of government, in which a rough-and-ready set of checks and balances maintained a high level of personal freedom and opportunity for individuals.

GREAT STATESMAN

William Pitt the Elder, Earl of Chatham (1708–78), came from a talented but wildly temperamental family. His dramatic oratory made him powerful in the House of Commons and popular with the merchant community. He fiercely supported Britain's trading and colonial interests. He was an inspired war leader: under his direction British forces swept the French from India, Canada and the West Indies.

ABOVE LEFT: Aristocratic government – Sir Robert Walpole and his cabinet. The expression on the face of the bishop at the right of the picture suggests the First Lord of the Treasury is telling one of his famous bawdy stories.

RIGHT: A cartoon by Thomas Rowlandson of the parliamentary election in 1784. Society ladies became actively involved in the campaign, to the ribald amusement of all and sundry.

ABOVE: William Pitt the Younger addressing the House of Commons in 1793. He was practically a child prodigy as a politician, becoming Prime Minister at the age of 24, but he expended most of his energy in a long, defensive struggle against revolutionary France.

RIGHT: Hogarth's famous cartoon of John Wilkes presents the radical politician as an incarnation of leering malice, with a hint of the devil. To his supporters, however, he was a heroic defender of constitutional liberties.

AN ECONOMIC EXPLOSION

*T*HE BRITISH ECONOMY WAS transformed in the 18th century, and with it the lifestyles and expectations of the inhabitants of the British Isles. All of Britain's subsequent prosperity has rested, in fact, on the foundations laid in the Georgian period.

There was no one single cause of this economic success story; rather, there was a cluster of inter-related factors. Population growth began in the early part of the century, when landowners, enriched by new sources of capital, some of it won from foreign

trade, were able to improve their farms sufficiently to feed a small but statistically crucial increase in the child population. This expanding population both inflated demand for industrial produce and, by its labour, made possible a startling growth in national productivity.

Finally, both the raw materials for industry and the finished goods which resulted were moved around the country with increasing ease

LEFT: *The world's first iron bridge was built across the River Severn near Coalbrookdale in 1779 and gave its name to the town of Ironbridge. Coalbrookdale was the site of the first large-scale iron smelting works.*

LEFT: This iron forge is still being run as a family cottage industry. Elsewhere the production of iron and steel was being developed on a much larger scale.

RIGHT: Richard Arkwright claimed credit for inventing the spinning machine which transformed the cotton and woollen industries, but his real originality lay in grouping machines so that they could be driven by water and steam power – the beginnings of the factory system.

and speed as the growth of wealth enabled enterprising individuals to build networks of canals and roads.

In rough figures, Britain's population rose from 5.8 million in 1700, to 10.5 million in 1800; her agricultural productivity increased by half, her overseas trade quadrupled, and her industrial capacity increased five times, while 2,300 miles (3,680 kilometres) of canals and about 22,000 miles (35,000 kilometres) of roads were constructed.

This complex outburst of economic activity resembled a shot fired into a powder magazine; demand and supply fuelled each other, creating ever-greater explosions that continue to resound today.

BELOW LEFT: The fields around the manor house at Dixton, Gloucestershire, have been enclosed and are being worked in the approved 18th-century manner. Agriculture, organised around the estates of the gentry, was the basis of the economy.

WEDGWOOD POTTERY

Josiah Wedgwood had little education and only about £20 of capital when he set up on his own as a potter in 1760. He was technically both skilled and inventive, however, and improved his talent by studying classical work. He was a masterly organiser who made full use of developments in water-borne transport to avoid the bumpy roads and whose astute management of finance and labour laid the foundation of the factory system.

ENTERPRISE AND EMPIRE

THE BRITISH EMPIRE IN THE 18th century was based on sea-borne trade. In this it was quite different from the accumulation of territories acquired by British military effort and administered by means of railway networks in the 19th century, and still more different from the global confederation which briefly dominated world politics in the first half of the 20th century.

Colonies, to the merchant adventurers of 18th-century London and Bristol, were simply sources of goods – exotic products such as sugar from the West Indies, tobacco from Virginia, spices from the East Indies, furs from Canada or tea from China; or items of value to be had in trade with the locals – pearls and precious stones,

silks and porcelain. Only the Thirteen Colonies that later became the founding elements of the United States of America departed from the norm by developing increasingly as colonies of settlement; significantly, they were the first to break away from the mother country, in the War of American Independence (1775–83).

Britain's great rival in the competition for world trade was France; the victim of both was Spain, an ailing power. It was a triangular relationship, which took a coldly diplomatic, formally military shape in successive European wars, particularly the War of the Spanish Succession (1701–14), the War of the Quadruple Alliance (1718–20) and the War of the Austrian Succession (1740–48).

In a less organised manner, hostilities broke out in fierce and uncoordinated violence on all the oceans and distant coastlines of the world, at erratic times throughout the century; the Seven Years' War, fought against the French in North America between 1756 and 1763, is an example of one such conflict.

LEFT: The growth of British trade with China gave rise to a fashionable craze for all things Chinese. This design by Sir William Chambers for the Pagoda in Kew Gardens dates from about 1761.

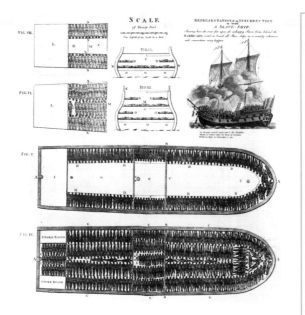

RIGHT: This diagram of a slave ship shows how the slaves were ruthlessly packed on to racks on each deck.

OPPOSITE BELOW: A triumphal moment in the career of Robert Clive (1725–74), founder of the British Empire in India. In this painting, Clive receives the right to manage the taxes in Bengal from its Indian ruler, in 1765.

THE SOUTH SEA BUBBLE

In 1720 the South Sea Company offered to take over three-fifths of the National Debt as an investment which it hoped to recoup by trading under government licence with South America. There was a speculative rush to invest in South Sea shares, which rapidly rose tenfold in value. Within weeks, however, confidence had collapsed: investors lost all their money, the company collapsed and the government went down with the wreck.

BELOW: The port of Bristol in the 18th century was booming due to a triangular trade – European manufactured goods to Africa, African slaves to the West Indies, and West Indian sugar, tobacco and cotton to Britain.

DEFINING THE NATION

THE NATION THAT EMERGED from 18th-century Britain forged its identity largely through opposition and conflict.

The abolition of the Scottish Parliament in 1707 under the terms of the union of the two kingdoms was much resented at first in Scotland, but soon came to be seen as conveying advantages and opportunities that had not been possible before. The attempted Jacobite coups of 1715 and 1745 embittered relations between the Scots and English for much of the century, but by 1805 matters had so altered that one Scottish MP, David Scott, was able to urge that Scots should 'never be offended with the word English being applied in future to express any of his majesty's subjects' – a view which, one might think, no Scottish politician would advocate now. Unification was also aided by inter-marriage between the English and Scottish aristocracies in the second half of the 18th century, with much the same process going on in Wales and in Ireland at the same time.

THE GREAT ADMIRAL

Of all Englishmen, Horatio Nelson (1758–1805) has perhaps been the most idolised. From 1793 onwards, he played a prominent part in the naval war against France until, in 1805, he defeated the combined fleets of France and Spain at Trafalgar, destroying forever Napoleon's hopes of transporting an army to attack Britain. He was mortally wounded in his famous last battle and his body was brought home for burial in St Paul's Cathedral.

ABOVE: The French fortress of Quebec in Canada, impregnable until General James Wolfe captured it by a daring surprise attack at dawn on 13 September 1759.

LEFT: *The 'Boston Tea Party' of 16 December 1773, when American colonists threw chests of tea into Boston harbour, was a protest against the imposition of taxes and duties by the government in London and led eventually to the colonies' independence.*

One of the main underlying forces motivating the process of national unification was the prolonged struggle with France, and the effort required to seize and hold an empire abroad. This conflict engaged the energies of all the most dynamic elements in British society. What was so remarkable about generals such as Clive and Wolfe, and the serried ranks of Scottish engineers and Irish adventurers, was that their pursuit of private profit gave rise, time and again, to a powerful British patriotism, frequently expressed in terms of the loftiest idealism.

ABOVE: *The Battle of Culloden in 1746 ended the last serious attempt by the Stuart dynasty to reclaim the British throne. The Duke of Cumberland's well-equipped army defeated Prince Charles Edward Stuart's brave but undisciplined rabble.*

RIGHT: *Sir Thomas Lawrence's magnificent portrait of the Duke of Wellington as a confident, masterful soldier at the height of his professional powers.*

A Cosmopolitan Aristocracy

THE ARISTOCRACY OF EUROPE enjoyed its golden age in the 18th century, when even the most powerful and active monarchs relied on their nobilities to manage affairs for them, fight their wars and police the peasantry. What we now call 'the state' was comprised in the 18th century, quite simply, of the nobility – the politicians, generals and judges who were the effective governors of the estates whose names they bore as titles.

Nowhere was the aristocracy wealthier, more powerful or more successful than in Britain. Land was the basis of their position, and their motto might have been 'what we have, we hold'. By the end of the 18th century, the custom of inheritance by the eldest son, combined with an unusually high rate of child-lessness among the aristocracy, had consoli-dated much of the British Isles in the hands of a few hundred families.

Yet there was also a strongly international flavour to the British aristocracy. Much of this was due to French cultural pre-eminence, a fact acknowledged in manners, costumes and language – the use of French was a defining mark of politeness on any social occasion.

ABOVE: An Elegant Family Taking Tea, *by Gavin Hamilton. 'Politeness conjures up some familiar features of Georgian society . . . its faith in a measured code of manners, its attachment to elegance and stateliness . . .' (Paul Langford).*

LEFT: British gentlemen on the Grand Tour view the antiquities of Rome.

The custom of the Grand Tour, which was almost *de rigueur* among young British aristocrats until rudely disrupted by the savageries of the French Revolution, was a rite of initiation into the European caste. Chaperoned by a tutor, usually a compliant clergyman, the young nobleman would tour Italy and the German states and above all would pay tribute at Versailles, collecting curios, works of art, manners and polish, before returning to adorn his family mansion with the trophies of his wanderings.

ROBERT ADAM

Robert Adam and his brother James were the most fashionable architects and interior designers working in England and Scotland during the second half of the 18th century. They built both country mansions and town houses, large and small, and designed much furniture and fittings for the houses which they planned. They used elegantly restrained motifs with fresh, strong colour schemes, all carefully related to classical originals.

AN ARCHITECTURE OF ASSERTION

*E*IGHTEENTH-CENTURY ARISTOCRATS had a passion for building. The century opened to the sound of baroque trumpets as Sir John Vanbrugh designed and built the stupendous palaces of Blenheim and Castle Howard, for the Duke of Marlborough and the Earl of Carlisle respectively. These were triumphant assertions of grandeur, conceived and executed on a gigantic scale and set in landscapes that were re-shaped and modelled as far as the eye could see. Blenheim in particular, the gift of a grateful state to its greatest general, was a statement of national as well as personal pride. Architecture on such a grand scale was rare, but aristocratic families, and those who wished to be numbered among the aristocracy, built houses, such as the Bathursts' Cirencester Park in Gloucestershire and the Cokes' Holkham Hall in Norfolk, to proclaim their owners' social supremacy over the locality. The great house built by the Temple family at Stowe in Buckinghamshire was, still more, the headquarters of a Whig faction whose influence persisted over several generations. In comparison with Stowe,

BELOW: Blenheim Palace was designed by Sir John Vanbrugh and built for the 1st Duke of Marlborough by the nation in recognition of his victory at Blenheim.

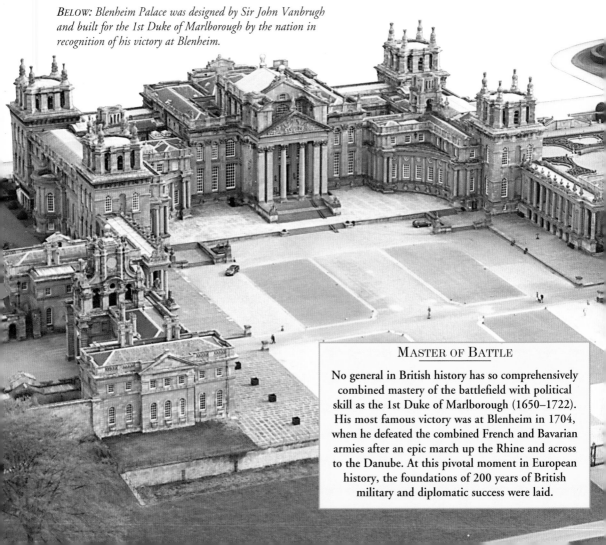

MASTER OF BATTLE

No general in British history has so comprehensively combined mastery of the battlefield with political skill as the 1st Duke of Marlborough (1650–1722). His most famous victory was at Blenheim in 1704, when he defeated the combined French and Bavarian armies after an epic march up the Rhine and across to the Danube. At this pivotal moment in European history, the foundations of 200 years of British military and diplomatic success were laid.

RIGHT: The garden front of Castle Howard, Yorkshire, by Sir John Vanbrugh. Horace Walpole wrote of Castle Howard, 'I have seen gigantic palaces before, but never a sublime one'.

Houghton Hall in Norfolk, the house built by the most successful of all 18th-century politicians, Sir Robert Walpole, seems compact and austere.

To the modern visitor these 'stately houses' can seem like museums, but for the first occupants they were family homes, and much more besides – estate offices, the headquarters of political and business concerns, centres of learning and the arts (Pope translated Homer at Stanton Harcourt, Turner lived and painted at Petworth, in each case as guests of the noble owners). The houses swarmed with servants, children and animals, and were almost self-contained villages, which provided jobs and security for many people.

ABOVE: Several architects played their part in creating Stowe and its temple-studded parkland in Buckinghamshire. The coldly magnificent south front with its haughty portico was the work of Robert Adam.

ABOVE: William Kent built Holkham Hall in Norfolk for the Earl of Leicester, who collected Roman antiquities. The entrance hall and staircase are in the Roman-inspired Palladian style of architecture which was popular in Britain in the middle of the 18th century.

LEFT: Harewood House, Yorkshire, designed by John Carr of York. J.M.W. Turner's view of the house from the south-east shows it commanding and splendid, but wholly at ease in its rolling parkland.

CIVILISING NATURE

MANY OF THE FEATURES WHICH we take for granted as natural elements of the English countryside were created by landowners and farmers in the 18th century. The chequerboard of small to medium-sized fields, surrounded by hedges, was produced by enclosing the huge ploughlands and commons that surrounded English villages in the Midland counties until the late 17th century.

The rolling parks, often hundreds of acres in extent, that surrounded the great houses were designed, like the farmers' agricultural enclosures, to protect the security of private property, maximise efficiency of management and satisfy the century's passion for order. Within the park walls, streams were dammed to form lakes, trees were planted in belts and groves to shelter game, and ornamental features – columns, obelisks, statues, pavilions, arbours, temples, terraces, artificial ruins – were constructed to please the eye.

At the beginning of the century, fashionable notions about what constituted the ideal landscape around a great house were dominated

RIGHT: The Palladian bridge at Stowe is an elegant imitation of the bridge at Wilton, which in turn was derived from a classical original.

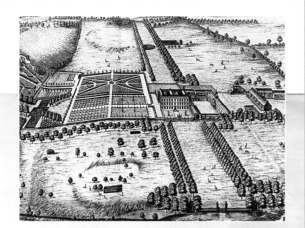

Lancelot 'Capability' Brown (1715–83) – so called because of his habit of professing to find 'great capability of improvement' in any park or garden that he was invited to view – created the English parkland ideal of grand sweeps and vistas. This portrait by Richard Cosway suggests a practical, purposeful man of business.

ABOVE LEFT: The formal gardens, the spreading parkland with deer and the long avenue up to Hammels, in Hertfordshire, all emphasise the haughty power of its 18th-century owners.

LEFT: All the greatest gardeners of the 18th century – William Kent, 'Capability' Brown and Humphrey Repton – worked in turn on the gardens of Wilton House, the seat of the Earl of Pembroke, near Salisbury.

by French or Dutch practice, in which orderly parades of well-pruned and shaped trees or hedges marched along straight avenues to a geometrically regular expanse of ornamental water. From the mid-century onwards, however, formality fell out of vogue.

First came the naturalism of Lancelot 'Capability' Brown who abandoned straight lines for curves in his planting, and aimed both to smooth and to enhance whatever natural features he found. Brown's simplicity was superseded by the romanticising tendencies of Humphrey Repton, who was willing to create interest where none existed. Their creations and those of their followers set a style which dominated European taste in landscape design for more than 150 years.

THE GROWTH OF TOWNS

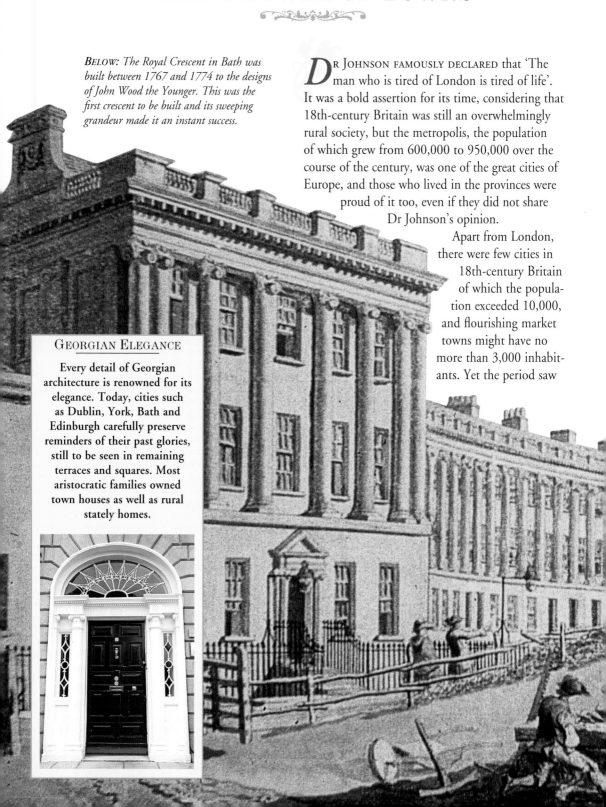

BELOW: The Royal Crescent in Bath was built between 1767 and 1774 to the designs of John Wood the Younger. This was the first crescent to be built and its sweeping grandeur made it an instant success.

GEORGIAN ELEGANCE

Every detail of Georgian architecture is renowned for its elegance. Today, cities such as Dublin, York, Bath and Edinburgh carefully preserve reminders of their past glories, still to be seen in remaining terraces and squares. Most aristocratic families owned town houses as well as rural stately homes.

DR JOHNSON FAMOUSLY DECLARED that 'The man who is tired of London is tired of life'. It was a bold assertion for its time, considering that 18th-century Britain was still an overwhelmingly rural society, but the metropolis, the population of which grew from 600,000 to 950,000 over the course of the century, was one of the great cities of Europe, and those who lived in the provinces were proud of it too, even if they did not share Dr Johnson's opinion.

Apart from London, there were few cities in 18th-century Britain of which the population exceeded 10,000, and flourishing market towns might have no more than 3,000 inhabitants. Yet the period saw

RIGHT: Robert Adam designed the north side of Charlotte Square in Edinburgh but died before the rest of the square, part of Edinburgh's New Town, was completed.

a significant growth in the urban population. Many of the new town-dwellers were poor immigrants from the countryside, who found what lodgings they could in the disease-infested, crime-ridden rookeries that were a feature of all large centres of population in 18th-century Europe. But many others, particularly the newly prosperous middle classes, lived in a comfort unknown since Roman times.

To meet their demands, terraces of handsome houses were set beside paved streets, which were graced by public buildings – churches, inns, law courts, market halls, assembly rooms and theatres – of incomparable splendour and elegance. Bath, Dublin and the New Town of Edinburgh were admired by visitors from all over Europe, and it says much for the attractions of 18th-century London that the great Canaletto was willing to spend ten of the best years of his life painting its buildings, rather than those of his native Venice.

ABOVE: London advances into the countryside – the terraces of Islington thrust out into the hayfields of Canonbury in this engraving of 1787.

SOCIALISING

TOWNS IN 18TH-CENTURY Britain were predominantly trading and meeting-places – the concept of the industrial town as a manu-facturing-place came with the spread of steam-power and the growth of the factory system in the 19th century.

The rich regarded them-selves as country-dwellers. Their great houses or 'seats' were to be found at the heart of their rural estates rather than in cities, and they regularly spent a significant part of each year in the country, either when the weather in town was too hot for comfort, or when the pleasures of country sports beckoned.

As roads and carriages improved, however, it became more and more fashionable and convenient for those with any social pretensions to visit London, or a provincial capital such as Edinburgh, Dublin, York or Exeter. They came to attend the theatre or the concert hall, to take part in balls and similar entertainments, and to follow the fashionable, highly formal

ABOVE: A scene in Vauxhall Gardens, London, in 1808. Pleasure gardens such as Vauxhall provided entertainment for the fashionable classes and hangers-on. At best, they were places of enchantment, but some were very tawdry.

BELOW: Not everyone went to Bath in search of a cure – fashionable society flocked there for amusements of all sorts, including the opportunity for their daughters to meet suitable gentlemen.

A London coffee house in about 1705. These establishments, where men met over the newly fashionable drink, quickly came to provide opportunities for business, politics or literary activities as well as socialising. Some of them turned into City institutions, others spawned newspapers and journals, and others again became the political and social clubs of the West End.

ABOVE: The Georgians enjoyed eating huge quantities of food. The table in the dining room of Fairfax House in York is laid for the first course of a meal as served in 1763.

rounds of visits and receptions at which their manners, costumes and conversations could be displayed to best advantage.

The men relaxed in the coffee houses, or, later in the century, in gentlemen's clubs, such as White's, Brook's or Boodle's, some of which were devoted to gambling and others to more sedate pleasures. The women ruled the Assembly Rooms, which adorned even the most modest provincial towns – spacious, elegant chambers, where receptions and parties provided entertainment and opportunities to capture a husband, the motivation for much of the ceremonious socialising.

And then, when over-loaded digestions began to complain, it was time for a trip to Bath, with its health-giving spa and a fresh round of concerts, plays, receptions, and fashionable services in the abbey, where the walls were already crowded with the memorial tablets of those who had come to take the waters and never left.

HIGH LIFE AND LOW LIFE

THE MOOD OF THE TIMES was all in favour of reason, balance, moderation and calm – yet the social life of 18th-century Britain was marked by every sort of extreme.

It was a violent society, in which savage crimes such as murder and rape were common; duelling was a feature of aristocratic high life, while highway robbery was a common resort of the desperate poor; all classes engaged gleefully in brutal sports from bear-baiting and cock-fighting to bare-knuckle boxing. Public executions were popular entertainment.

Gambling was a near-universal mania, for stakes that might amount to a man's life-resources on a single throw; 'The young men lose five, ten, fifteen thousand pounds in an evening', wrote Horace Walpole. 'Lord Stavordale . . . lost eleven thousand last Tuesday, but recovered it by one great hand of hazard'.

Alcohol was consumed on a gargantuan scale; cheap gin devastated the lives of the London poor in the 1740s, when it was said that tavern signs advertised 'Drunk for a 1d, Dead Drunk for 2d'. Sexual promiscuity was a male privilege which, however, required the co-operation of a large proportion of the female population. Venereal disease was rampant in all groups of society, and was reckoned by contemporaries to be one of the principal checks on the growth of the population.

All these vices were characteristics of a society which, at the same time, exhibited more polish, refinement, sophistication, elegance and rational human-ity than any that the world had seen before. Life in Georgian Britain can rarely have been dull!

CRIME AND PUNISHMENT

Georgian society believed that growing wealth was matched by a rise in crime. The response was savage: between 1688 and 1820 the number of capital offences grew from about 50 to over 200 since public hangings were thought to have a deterrent effect, and relatively small offences were punished by transportation to North America. Reformers such as John Howard, however, urged the need for humane policies including prisons as reformatories rather than dungeons of despair.

LEFT: Cock-fighting was immensely popular with all classes. Specially bred birds, equipped with long steel spurs, were incited to fight to the death and large sums were frequently wagered on the result.

BELOW: William Hogarth's famous print of 'Gin Lane', published in 1750, is probably political propaganda rather than accurate observation. However, a ready supply of cheap gin undoubtedly wreaked appalling ravages on London's poor.

LEFT: Most of the tales about Dick Turpin, the famous highwayman hanged at York in 1739, were little more than legend. Highway robbers tended to be glamorised as 'gentlemen of the road', who plundered the rich with dashing gallantry.

SPLENDOUR AND SOPHISTICATION

For those 18th-century men and women who could afford it, the achievement of a splendid, or at least an elegant, personal appearance was practically an art form in itself. Fashion in costume was dominated for much of the century by French influence. Clothes for men had much of the quality of uniform – farmers, professional men, soldiers and noblemen would each dress the part. Hairstyles were more or less elaborate for both sexes, though men's wigs gradually became simpler until they were eventually discarded. Scent was much used by both sexes to compensate for the practical difficulties of taking a bath.

Fashions in furniture were robust and durable, to suit the needs of a nation of heavy drinkers and hard sportsmen. The names of Chippendale and Sheraton still carry an assurance of quality in design and workmanship today.

RIGHT: A fashion plate of 1807 showing the simpler lines of women's dress that came into vogue in Britain after the French Revolution.

Among other arts which flourished in Georgian Britain, those of the silversmith, the clockmaker and the glass-blower were especially notable. One of the greatest of all silversmiths was Hester Bateman, whose work is satisfyingly elegant and authoritative. John Harrison's clocks, designed to deliver the unfailing accuracy required for the calculation of longitude at sea, set new standards in horology. Glass from Waterford was one of many contributions made by 18th-century Ireland to the luxury of Georgian Britain.

The nation's musical life, which at the beginning of the century had a vigorous British flavour handed down from Purcell and Boyce, became increasingly dominated by German influences, particularly George Frederick Handel, perhaps the most naturalised German ever to have come to the British Isles.

RIGHT: A hairdresser tends to milady's coiffure, from Hogarth's satirical sequence 'Marriage à la mode'. French hairdressers were much in demand throughout the century, at least among the ladies.

Music was highly valued and widely practised in the Georgian period. The Sharp family (above), as painted by Johann Zoffany, was evidently proud of its musical accomplishments – between them they seem to have played almost every instrument available at the time. The extraordinary wind instrument held by the man in the cocked hat on the left is a serpent.

ABOVE: With its ivory inlay and nobility of line, this cupboard – the Diana and Minerva Commode, from Harewood House – has been described as Thomas Chippendale's finest creation.

RIGHT: A silver basket by the French silversmith Paul de Lamerie, whose work was popular among the wealthy in Georgian Britain.

CROWNING GLORIES

THE GEORGIAN PERIOD WAS the Golden Age of British painting. William Hogarth, with his consummate draughtsmanship and social insights, the equestrian painter Stubbs, and John Constable, who depicted the quiet beauties of the countryside, stood among the world's great artists, while Gainsborough, Lawrence, Ramsay and Raeburn were leading lights in a school of portraitists which was headed by the brilliant Sir Joshua Reynolds.

But it seems always to have been in literature that the British – and especially the English – artistic sensibility has expressed itself most effectively. The 18th century produced the poets Pope, Cowper and Gray, and dramatists Sheridan and Goldsmith, while in Dr Johnson's hands the craft of literary criticism was elevated into a high and lofty art. But the greatest literary achievement of the 18th-century was the 'invention' of the novel, which began with Defoe and Swift, passed on through Richardson, Smollett, Fielding and Sterne to excel in the works of Jane Austen.

BELOW: This scene from Henry Fielding's novel Tom Jones *was painted by the 19th-century artist Michael Angelo Rooker and shows a romanticised view of the period, and of the earthy, ribald masterpiece.*

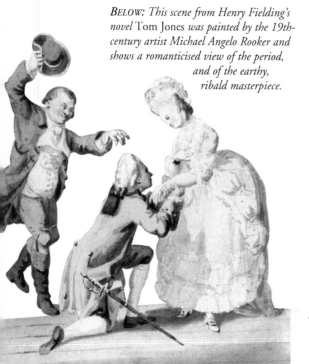

There is a paradox in the fact that the works of many of these painters and writers, while acknowledged as a high point in the history of British culture, are almost neglected today. The same may, perhaps, be said for the 18th century as a whole – a period of innovation and enterprise which made possible the teeming achievements of the 19th century, but which is all too often dismissed as 'difficult' and irrelevant.

JANE AUSTEN

This portrait of the novelist from a sketch by her sister Cassandra shows Jane Austen as the quiet daughter of a country clergyman, but one with a sharply observant eye. Her novels deal with ordinary people and situations, but her psychological insight, exquisite prose and subtle irony render them immediately compelling. Four of her novels were published anonymously during her lifetime and two under her signature after her death in 1817.

ABOVE: Dr Samuel Johnson (1709–84) by Sir Joshua Reynolds. Johnson was known as an essayist, political writer, poet, moralist, conversationalist and compiler of the first famous dictionary of the English language.

LEFT: Thomas Gainsborough's portrait of himself with his wife and daughter is both simple and candid.

Towards the end of the 18th century a revolutionary spirit was stirring, in literature as in political thought. Radical notions influenced a 'new wave' of Romantic writers. The poets William Wordsworth and Samuel Taylor Coleridge published *Lyrical Ballads* in 1798; their mission, inspired by nature and 'feeling' rather than by the classical works of antiquity, was to transmute common experience into eternal verities. The Romantic movement inspired other writers such as Keats, Shelley and Byron, and was inclined to favour emotion and individualism over reason and social convention. As the 18th century closed, the social and intellectual order that had held throughout most of the Georgian era was giving way to a new age of reform, scientific materialism, factories, railways and steam engines - the Britain of empire and industry.

LEFT: A fireworks display in Green Park, for which Handel composed music, to celebrate the peace of Aix-la-Chapelle, 1748. Georgian Britain enjoyed its triumphs with uninhibited gusto!

Places To Visit

BRITAIN HAS A WEALTH of fine Georgian houses and gardens. Some are in public ownership, others are privately owned, but most are open to the public for at least some days in the year. Here are contact details for a selection of just some of those that are well worth a visit.

Assembly Rooms and Fashion Museum, Bennett Street, Bath, Somerset BA1 2QH, 01225 477 789, www.nationaltrust.org.uk/main/w-bathassembly rooms **NT**

Blenheim Palace, Woodstock, Oxfordshire OX20 1PX, 01993 810500, www.blenheimpalace.com

Bowood House, Calne, Wiltshire SN11 0LZ, 01249 812102, www.bowood-house.co.uk

Castle Howard, York YO60 7DA, 01653 648333, www.castlehoward.co.uk

Chatsworth House, Bakewell, Derbyshire DE45 1PP, 01246 565300, www-chatsworth.org

Erddig Hall, Erddig, Wrexham LL13 0YT, 01978 355314, www.nationaltrust.org.uk/main/w-erddig **NT**

Fairfax House, Castle Gate, York, North Yorkshire YO1 9RN, 01904 655543, www.fairfaxhouse.co.uk

The Georgian House (museum)**,** 7 Charlotte Square, Edinburgh EH2 4DR, 0844 493 2118, www.nts.org.uk/Property/56 **NTS**

Harewood House, Harewood, Leeds, West Yorkshire LS17 9LG, 0113 218 1010, www.harewood.org

Holkham Hall, Wells-next-the-Sea, Norfolk NR23 1AB, 01328 710227, www.holkham.co.uk

Jane Austen's House Museum, Chawton, Alton, Hampshire GU34 1SD, 01420 83262, www.jane-austens-house-museum.org.uk

Kedleston Hall, Derby, Derbyshire DE22 5JH, 01332 842 191, www.nationaltrust.org.uk/main/w-kedlestonhall **NT**

Kenwood House, Hampstead Lane, London NW3 7JR, 020 8348 1286, www.englishheritage.org.uk/daysout/properties/kenwood-house **EH**

Kew Palace, 33 Kew Green, Richmond, Surrey TW9 3AB, 0844 4827777, www.hrp.org.uk/kewpalace

No. 1 Royal Crescent, Bath, Somerset BA1 2LR, 01225 428 126, www.bath-preservation-trust.org.uk/?id=3

Petworth House, Petworth, West Sussex GU28 0AE, 01798 343929, www.nationaltrust.org.uk/main/w-petworthhouse **NT**

Polesden Lacey, Great Bookham, near Dorking, Surrey RH5 6BD, 01372 458203, www.nationaltrust.org.uk/main/w-polesdenlacey **NT**

Stourhead Gardens, Stourton, Wiltshire BA12 6QD, 01747 841152, www.nationaltrust.org.uk/main/w-stourhead **NT**

Stowe Landscape Gardens, Buckingham, Buckinghamshire MK18 5DQ, 01494 755568, www.nationaltrust.org.uk/main/w-stowegardens **NT**

Wilton House, Wilton, Salisbury, Wiltshire SP2 0BJ, 01722 746700, www.wiltonhouse.com

Key to Symbols

EH English Heritage
NT National Trust
NTS National Trust for Scotland

Information correct at time of going to press.